MEIR CARROT

AND

THE HAPPY SHOP

To my lovely family
- M.B.

To Tom, Taiyo and Leo
- Mom S.

ISBN: 5-0-92912-965-978
Published by Madelaine Black
www.madelaineblack.com

MEIR CARROT

AND

THE HAPPY SHOPPER

Madelaine Black | Illustrations: Shirley Waisman

This is the tale of an Imma and son.
It's a story that could happen to anyone.
It should make you happy, so please don't feel down,
I'm sure there's a Food Bank right here in your town.

Imma kissed Danny, “Good morning my dear.”
Danny snapped: “There is nothing for breakfast in here.”
He drained the milk carton of its final drop,
Then poured in the last few cornflakes – plop, plop, plop!

Danny complained: “We’ve so little to eat!
Let’s go to the Food Bank that’s just down our street?
Mrs Friedman goes there every Tuesday at ten.
She gets bags of food, and spends time with her friends.”

“I cannot go there.” Imma groaned in a mood.
“Mrs Friedman needs it much more than we do.
I will not take help. We’ll manage. We’ll be fine.
I won’t go to that Food Bank, and wait in that line!”

Next day Imma said: “There is no need to fear.
I called the Food Bank and said we’ll volunteer.
Their yard will be filled with farm produce in crates.
We’ll help sort and pack it. We mustn’t be late.

The Food Bank opens for Shoppers at ten,
And food that’s donated is given to them.
I’ll ask Manager Ilanit if it’s OK
To take some food home, even though we can’t pay”.

Food Bank day has finally arrived.
Manager Ilanit's been there since five.
Danny watched the big trucks deliver fresh fare,
And volunteers sort it and bag it with care.

Danny picked up a pepper that fell on the ground,
When he heard voices sing a melodious sound.

"We've been planted, we've been grown.
Pack us, cook us, take us home!
Enjoy us any way you choose.
We're your Happy Shopper food!"

Danny looked in a crate that he thought was forgotten.
There lay a carrot and onion at the bottom.
Meir Carrot was yelling: “Take me home someone!”
Mrs Onion screamed: “My Little Onions have gone!”

“Imma, please help us!” Some sweet voices cried.
Danny peeped in a bag. There they were, safe inside.
“Here are your Little Onions!” Danny yelled out, excited.
So they and Mrs. Onion reunited.

Meir Carrot said to Danny: “Give this bag to your Imma.
To take home with you, and to use for your dinner.
We’ll all be so happy to cook in your pot.
You could make orange soup that’s delicious and hot!”

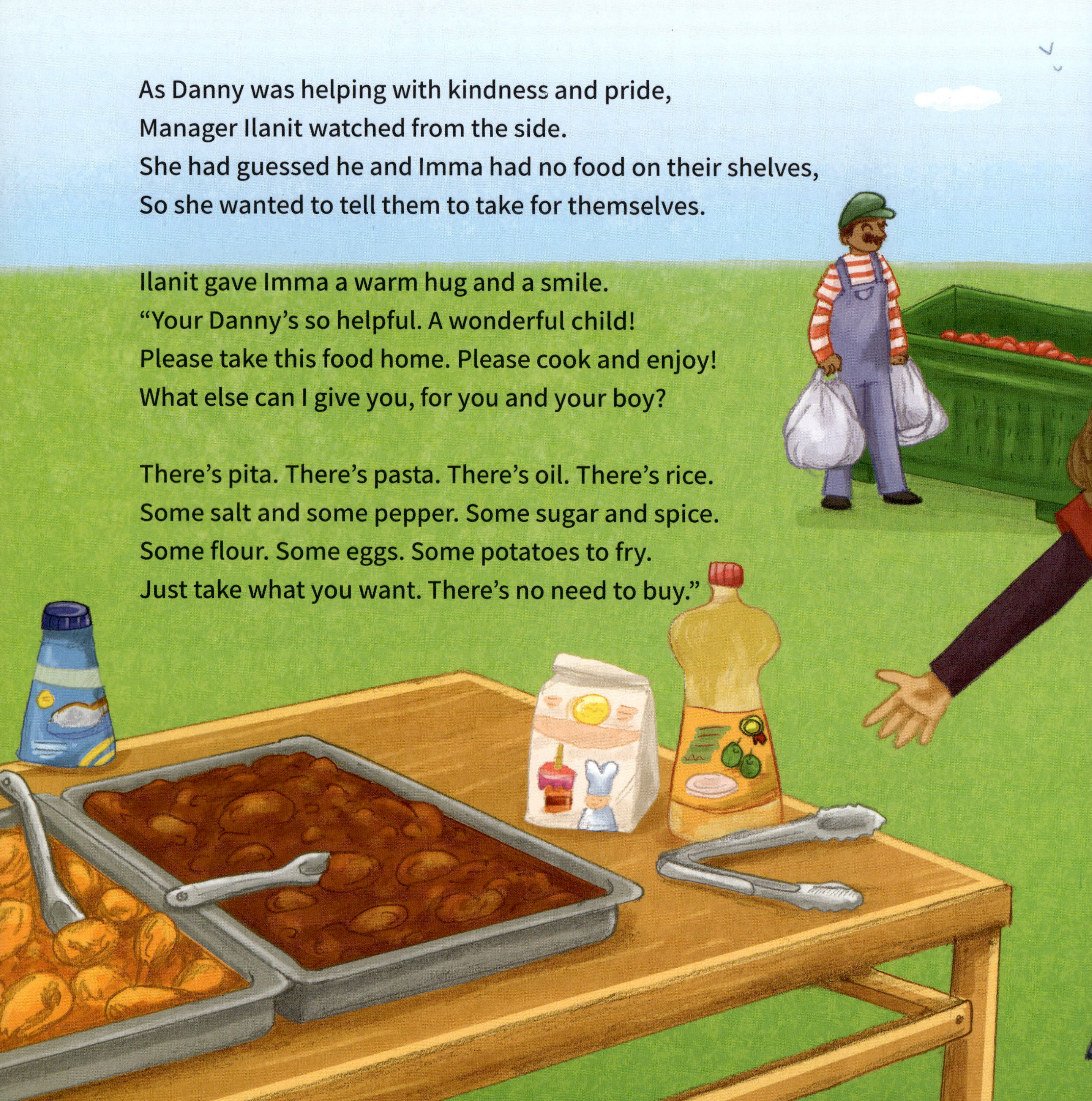

As Danny was helping with kindness and pride,
Manager Ilanit watched from the side.
She had guessed he and Imma had no food on their shelves,
So she wanted to tell them to take for themselves.

Ilanit gave Imma a warm hug and a smile.
"Your Danny's so helpful. A wonderful child!
Please take this food home. Please cook and enjoy!
What else can I give you, for you and your boy?

There's pita. There's pasta. There's oil. There's rice.
Some salt and some pepper. Some sugar and spice.
Some flour. Some eggs. Some potatoes to fry.
Just take what you want. There's no need to buy."

Danny and Imma walked home hand in hand.
Now they had food to eat, just as Imma had planned.
She no longer cared if someone would see them.
Then who should they meet in the street? Mrs Friedman!

"Danny, thanks so much for packing our wares!
Could you please help to take my bags up the stairs?
I've got chocolate to give you, my dear volunteer.
Thank God our Food Bank and its donors are here!"

Danny and Imma unloaded their food,
Excited to use it to cook something good.
Their favorite dish was fresh pasta and sauce.
With grated cheese sprinkled all over, of course!

“Snip snip” went the knife. “Scrape scrape” went the grater.”
They noshed as they cooked. They could not wait ‘til later.
”That Food Bank’s amazing.” Imma kissed Danny’s cheek.
“I won’t be so shy to go there next week.”

A delicious smell floated up into the air-
Fried onions and carrots for them both to share.
Whilst the spaghetti boiled Meir Carrot exclaimed:
"Danny, there's something I want to explain:

Whether fruit or vegetable, picker or packer,
Volunteer, Shopper, it just doesn't matter.
People give money. We all play our part.
We care for each other. We give from our heart.

In our wonderful country - rich with milk and honey-
No one should go hungry because they've no money.
Together. One family. We all are agreed.
Our Food Bank will give you the food that you need.

"We've been planted, we've been grown.
Pack us, cook us, take us home!
Enjoy us any way you choose.
We're your Happy Shopper food!"

About Food Banks

There are thousands of food banks all over the world, that each work in different ways.
Their goal is to help give food to people who do not have enough money to buy food for themselves.

This story is based on a real food bank in a town called Or Akiva in Israel. This food bank is run by an organization of caring people called Meir Panim. The name of the lovely manager at the food bank really is Ilanit!

Where does the food bank's food come from?

Each food bank has its own ways of getting food to give to people in need.
This food bank in Or Akiva gets their food in three main ways:

Food rescuers save fruits and vegetables that the farmers cannot pick, and then deliver them to the food bank.

Other food rescuers collect leftover, already cooked food from factories, stores, and restaurants.

People called "donors" give money to the food bank to buy food. "Volunteers" - people who give their time for free to do good things - come to the food bank to cook the food into tasty and healthy meals.

How is the food sorted and packed?

Trucks or food rescuers deliver the food to the food bank in boxes and big crates. Volunteers come and help to sort and pack the food into shopping bags, to give to the "shoppers".

Who are the shoppers?

The food bank team works very hard to find out who in the neighborhood does not have enough money to buy food for themselves and their family.
The food bank invites these people to come and receive food each week.

How do the shoppers receive their food?

The shoppers are welcomed to the food bank by workers and volunteers.

They are given bags of food already packed and ready to go.

They go home with bags of farm-fresh produce, and other foods- just like Danny and Imma in this story.

For more information, pictures, and videos about Meir Carrot and the food bank please take a look at www.meircarrot.com

About the Author

Madelaine Black's favorite thing to do is share funny stories and silly songs with her grandchildren.
Her other favorite thing to do is to help charities and non-profits to raise funds and awareness. She has spent 35 years in both the UK and Israel as an award-winning creative consultant. She calls what she does "creativity that matters".

The idea for this book about a magical talking carrot popped into Madelaine's head after an inspiring morning she spent volunteering at her local Meir Panim food bank.
www.madelaineblack.com

About the Illustrator

Shirley Waisman has illustrated more than fifty books for children. Her greatest reward is seeing children smiling as they enjoy her illustrations. Shirley grew up in Israel, and has been drawing and painting as long as she can remember. She studied her craft at the Bezalel Academy of Arts and Design and at Kyushu University, Japan.
www.shirleydesign.me

Special thanks and a big hug to Susan Coller